For John and Tim

THE
WATER
BEARER

TRACY RYAN

FREMANTLE PRESS

CONTENTS

THE
WATER
BEARER

TRACY RYAN

Tracy Ryan was born in Western Australia but has also lived in England, the United States and Ireland. She has worked in libraries, bookselling, editing, and community journalism, and has taught at various universities. She is especially interested in foreign languages and translation.

Previous poetry titles with Fremantle Press include *Unearthed, The Argument, Fremantle Poets 1: New Poets* (editor), *Scar Revision, Hothouse, The Willing Eye, Bluebeard in Drag* and *Killing Delilah*. Tracy Ryan is also the author of four novels: *Claustrophobia, Sweet, Jazz Tango* and *Vamp*. Her work has been commended in the National Book Council Banjo Award (1997), shortlisted in the Western Australian Premier's Book Awards (1994 and 1998), in *The Age* Book of the Year Award (2008) and the Adelaide Festival Awards for Literature (2012). She has won the *Australian Book Review* Poetry Prize (2009) and the Western Australian Premier's Book Awards (2000 and 2012).

Visit Tracy Ryan at poetsvegananarchistpacifist.blogspot.com

CAROUSEL

Dis, qu'as-tu fait, toi que voilà,
De ta jeunesse?
— Verlaine

Because in a foreign city even at eight
he needs the familiar nearby, to hitch
the gaze like the reins of that lacquered
horse to a fixed spot, in order to let loose,
someone to witness his flight or he can't
fully feel it, body forward but head turned
to the side, my side, he keeps me pinned here
on a bench at the roundabout's centre,
where I give back affirmation, looking out
from my still point, dead as a cyclone's eye.

I'm as much part of the furniture as each faceted
mirror, each Parisian pom-pom and oom-pa-pa,
mutely crucial like the unseen inner wheel
of the hurdy-gurdy, the curlicued chairs
and pastel tableaux where small folk-tale scenes
suffer grotesque encroachment but nevertheless
stay put, defying centrifugal force, I am what was
and he is what will be, launching eternally
into a churning future — over our heads it says
La Belle Epoque La Belle Epoque La Belle Epoque.

TRANSIT

Not even lifting a finger but with that swing
from walking, unconscious, palm open,
I catch it without volition, it catches me,
this white, minute feather, brush too aloof
to be called soft — but it did stop — weightless
as snowflake and just as blankly obvious,
the loss, the newness. Loose from a nest,
a fledgling, though there seemed
neither tree nor bird anywhere near me
to furnish it so listlessly, indifferently,
and I could not say what became of it
when it finished with me, glanced off,
as if it too might melt or dissipate, as if
without root in flesh or destination.

BERRIES IN SEPTEMBER

Some have been out
since we got here a month ago,
first cause for a motherly warning:
gorgeous, but you can't eat them.
He likes to walk by them, reminded
of Keats, one way of marking
this unfamiliar place, route to a new
school and home again, the poem
will cover a multitude of signs.
Yet now we see them everywhere
as if each street once reticent
were bursting to tell, were avid,
getting the berries up while
the going's good, sung like a red
and orange dispersal of swansong
or counterpoint, second cause, storm
before the calm; colour and opulence
insisting, they say: a bitter winter.

NEAR-EARTH OBJECTS

Built in is the possibility of it all going instantly.
Merely having a name seems minutest luxury, folly.

I'm still the open-mouthed child my brother could terrorise
by telling me the sun would end — will end, indeed

but so far along that the word *far*'s engulfed in
non-meaning the way the world would be. Will be.

And Tim, nearly nine now, who once lived for the sheer
idea of the mighty crab and horsehead nebulae —

something approaching God to him — hearing obliquely,
from a schoolmate, who's got slightly the wrong end

of partly the wrong stick, that a STAR today will crash into earth
turning us off like a switch before we're even aware of it

garbling, I guess, the story of NASA's cast-off six-tonne satellite
expected in twenty-six bits which could each pack

a substantial punch but at odds of twenty-one trillion to one,
can meet this great ontological mess only with *I hate space,*

I hate space.

THREE MICHAELMAS POEMS

in soft September, at slow, sad Michaelmas
— D.H. Lawrence

1. Equinox
Everything just on the edge, leaves
with the faintest flush of intimation
as if ashamed to admit defeat
though they should be used to it
and the sun soon reasserting itself to thwart
even satellite communication
before retreat, and the school's request
we donate some non-perishable item
to simulate, they say, an early form
of welfare provision, Christian and pagan.
A harvest — not a hunter's — moon.
No light to go out and ravage by,
no licence for appetite — instead
reminder of social obligation born
of abundance, a notion of balance.
Yet last night sharp shots kept
ringing out their lethal angelus
till we could only wish to picture
fireworks somewhere, a celebration.
Of an ending, a beginning.
I called the college porter
who said she couldn't hear them,
heard nothing. Next morning, a friend said:
military practice. Lucky the child's dread
slept through it — only because exhausted.

He's been learning the war in class and is
prone to translation, to taking things on.
Summer's as good as dead. I'm reading Lawrence,
the last, dark, steep decline of 'Bavarian Gentians'.

2. Effects

A kind of gleaning: the harvest is done
and you have moved on. Seasonal, nomadic.
I pick up the pieces, imagine them as
residual interface — this workspace,
virtual, collapsible as tent of Peri-Banou
— 'innate capacity for expanse' — a mortal
coil you'll not quite shuffle off despite
reincarnation 'like anyone starting a new life
in a country as foreign as this', you leave
(are always leaving) specific essentials,
cast-offs I might class as spartan, monastic:
means of coffee-making, reading, camping
or sleeping, shell-fragments I shall
move into, hermit crab, stick to the trail,
make part stand for whole, synecdochic
not static, museum-like, but pressed
into desperate service, like those objects
they give dogs, for sniffing out missing persons.

3. Underworld

Yesterday, in the dark basement of the University
Library, an exhibition — Books and Babies:
Communicating Reproduction.

Waiting to get my card,
magic of access — I faced down a gravid uterus engraved
in cross-section, 1774: the caption noted violence,
prurience, pride of display, as you might say, male
mastery. An image based on extensive dissection, even
the thighs of the purported woman in question cut
to the bone, to show we can.

On a screen
nearby, a looping documentary — *The Joy
of Sex Education* — with the sound turned down
on what appeared to be a hapless sixties chick
cradling telltale swelling, gazing on white-clad, green
eye-shadowed bride, aglow on the church steps.
Or maybe the two were one: they looked the same.

I'm reading Dreiser, a second time — his *Tragedy*,
and in that doubled girl I saw Roberta, the one likeable
doomed character, her lover-and-murderer sent to the chair
by the same state that denies her a termination.

Yesterday, in the world outside books, another execution.
I came up steps blinking into bright near-autumn.

14

THE BELLS

> *... the silence, wanly prinkt*
> *with forms of lingering notes*
> — Christopher Brennan

> *In Germany, there appear to have been few*
> *instances of overt resistance to the [Nazi]*
> *confiscation of church bells.*
> —Kirrily Freeman

I tilt the window
and they pour in here
cascading, swallowing
till I can't separate
sacred from secular —
how could it matter?
More than a marker
of time or collection
sanctus or death-knell
barely an interval
they take possession
with body and tongue.
Once they were named as
metallic resources.
Churches flew swastikas.
You can see photos
of the bell-graveyards
thousands awaiting
recasting for *service*
from all over Europe.
Now in Tübingen

they ring out in order:
some are survivors,
missed requisition
by virtue of heritage —
others too recent
to carry that weight.

SCHOOL WALK IN GERMAN WINTER

Our one star has departed
We're wholly dark
The clouds are shedding
Pretension to friendliness
Flake by flake
Which of us guides the other
Across this glassine surface
That blanks every letter
Deadening words
Who is that figure
Globe-headed, dirndl-skirted
Vacant hand-holder
The street-sign makes Mother
Her little familiar
When you were born
The ground had taken
More than a dusting
We were locked in
But not forever
Now you are thirteen
Age of *reversible prime*
And *happy number*
Of fact not rumour
Half-apprehended
Or superstition
Of getting up again
And walking onward
Of facing down
The downward forces
The *Niederschlag*

SMARTRAVELLER

Just knowing those colours makes it safer
already and how they'll change anyway by the time
you, thirteen now, are old enough for elsewhere:

Red Orange Yellow Green but not about weather
except for extremity and those are most finite
and fickle, cyclones though murderous rarely durable

as human cruelty. *Where are you going?*
the site prompts but you choose *Browse countries*
then *List all countries*, then run the current date —

not to miss anything — every day you check them
like a thing growing in the mind's garden
that needs tending, a world of worrying

for others under some degree of mastery; keep track
of flare-up, pandemic, earthquake, and ask me
sidelong, to define *civil unrest, safety and security*

though these are terms you know, as if rehearsing,
as if there could be something more the words don't
indicate, a further shade in my palette till now

held back, but I can only disappoint, being arm's length,
and listen my best as you list the ten tallest mountains
while we head for the school bus because last night

and all this week it was Nepal, and pulling your quilt
around you to ready for sleep was rugging up
for Everest, and before that, another land, one day.

WINTER: LIEBESTOD

Inured by now to snow
nothing could drag me
away from inwardness
this would-be scraping
and clearing of the mind's
dark drive with its slick
misnomer 'black' ice
to the neuralgic window —

except that queer aria
of howls, falsetto, which now
in counterpoint and now
in unison makes plaint
to a woman who not so much
walks two white dogs as is
herself spurred on by animal pain
and mine, and stops her ears.

WINCH-BIRD

Unseen, and named not by our utterance but by his own,
cranking the day up for me as he cranks your day down,
insistent and regular as the kitchen roller-shutter: *creak* ...
creak ... asserting particularity, necessity, marking off time
remaining in this place, staking out hours for work
and hours domestic, that querulous line between Home
and Them. The rest of the process a guessing-game,
if you care to determine who makes that mimic cry
and is endemic *and* does not leave in winter, allowing that
seasons are now so altered the guides don't always apply.
If we have to make him real I'll settle for *woodcock*,
Waldschnepfe, but in our private bird-world he will not
have to be hunted, only to be what he does, Winch-bird.

LAUBWALD

The yew keeps its green, and the distant pine.
All else is skeletal. We move through a huddle
of uprights, unidentifiable unless by branch or
bark but not being locally that literate, instead
we look to ground level, layer on layer of dried
discards that precede our time here, and noting
crimped contour say *Oak*, though no trunk quite
has that look, but the leaf is proof, even cast off,
there's continuity in being, compacting archive
we'd grind to nothing if not for the mud we want
to avoid, so we stick strictly to pathways, don't
digress despite soft invitation, keeping unmarked,
not wanting to shed the way this wood has shed,
refusing to own the ache, the creak, the chill in limb
and bone, we pass without seeming to pass, aware
our bareness too has dignity, with this difference,
the trees if let be will come good again, green again,
while we will be elsewhere, far, and not return.

ÖSTERBERG

Whether face-forward or over shoulder those
broken gables, open boxes with shutters like
spread pages impeccably legible, pitched against
yet holding each other upright, a lone raven
that hops across that steep snow-hip the only sign
of movement, that whole stack tacit but icily alert,
all apertures to catch you — each window looks onto
another window and there is no out of this *mise
en abyme*. Above them the remnant trees that stand
fast when all else is sliding, like the man whose bag-
handle snapped on his bicycle and left him gathering
cans and packets from the glazed gutter as others gazed
impassible, the little wood that has tidied away its loss
and wears its white as no hindrance, *this too shall pass*.

TILT-AND-TURN

The windows are uncountable
yet plural. On every outdoor
town-view, they dominate — also
singly, from inside, loom over us.
Hold threads under tension, a frame.
Edgy magic, they might unhinge,
fall inward. We *tilt* them back to air
the room for want of fan or vent,
releasing vapours, our humours.
Out there, commingled.
They gauge the day, admit
street-sound, anonymous.
No veil, this pane, no projection
of hymen, fantastic intactness;
it was always already open.
Not for *turning* your back on.
Nor for dreaming you live in
another's life. Rather for keeping
charge like *custodia fenestrarum*,
alone in a crowd, *turning* this blind
eye as I hoist or lower the sail.

NEXT TO GODLINESS

1. Oldtown made new

Out on the cobbles a man
with litter-stick skewers
leftovers from Fasnet's
fakery: confetti and smashed
boiled sweets, crock-like broken
bottles all into his sack while
a crazed woman walks beside him
crying *Ich weiß Ich weiß* and *Scheiße*

2. Houseweek

Day comes in, sits on the stairs
and will not sweep itself away

buttons and tags and instructions
paper the walls, your name is given up

to this machinic box that might even be
musical if you could find the crank-

handle, but what would it play?
You are inside and don't have an

overview, belong to the robotics
reminisce about slackness and mess

long for the dry dust that was at least
all yours, instead of leaf-pulp and other

people's slush, day sits on the stairs
in tatters and residues and the calendar,

through which alone you know your
neighbours, will have it otherwise

3. Cellar

Below the frost-line
it smells of earth and death
I must go down

where things unsightly
brood and cluster
no longer wanted

or else unseasonal
bide their time
till resurrection

I pass with trepidation
maimed chair and broken
bicycle, partial window

that lets in street voices
and feet at eye-level
and yet no light

a world inverted
or silent carnival
fixed on elimination

internal tangle
that snake-nest of piping
this line of meters

labelled with names
where everyone's plugged in
that padlocked stash

of wine maturing, still
anchored to the human, hideous
walls the whole thing's foundation.

4. Subcellar

But there is worse
and I have found it
a second, deeper level
of gated caves,
dungeons or catacombs
where I must leave
our leavings till collection day
things that are too far gone
for even a look-out basement
to tolerate, emptied hulls
and wrappings, caps and casings
all traces of person washed off
whistle-clean, bone-dry.

NOW LIE IN IT

Two single white quilts mark us out
neat as stone slabs, short of inscription —
we turn of our own volition, not subject

to each other's mood or movement
so different from long-worn habit!
At night, I no longer register when

you get up — we each have a bedside
light and the split in linen means
you're independent when you would

likely be most lost, straining for
water or glasses, your side is noiseless
but my far side croaks throatily

complains of someone heavier
someone who came before, living
their too-large life otherwise

than we do, than what we planned
or pictured when we signed up,
signed on, just as by day we go our

separate work-ways now, yet it was
we who made this choice and who will see
it through, while seeing through it

like any 'commitment', dreamily
reminiscent by darkness of easier times,
there must be more, there must be other

ways and places we'll find our way to
or way *back* to, nothing ever being
permanent, as they say, but change

SEHNSUCHT

I do not find you in the morning dark
when houses one by one awake
and might as well be empty

nor when each firefly bicycle
veers past me into equal uncertainty
you are not there to face the looming

faceless man who drops and then picks up
and carries his wrested lamp again
because it is less about seeing than about

being seen, a light that cries *Notice and do
not come near me*, carving a gleaming path
a lone trajectory that could be any

one of us, I do not touch you in the chill halo
that mounts along with each new passenger
on this bus, the cloud peculiar to every silently

elapsing life, a breath of death that wraps us
you might say, overlapped and sharing, only truly
communal in it, nor in the salve on lips and hands

day-long eaten down by the dominant, Winter,
no backdrop nor mere season, a central actor
in the scene where I cannot continue and yet

I do, though I do not find you here.

RAINER MARIA RILKE

LOVE SONG

How shall I still my soul so it won't stir
against your soul? How shall I lift it over
you, elevate it toward other things?
Oh, I would like to leave it with whatever
is lost and wasted in some unfamiliar
dark, hidden spot that never rings
in answer when your deepest places do.
Yet everything that touches me and you
takes us together in the way a bow-
stroke draws a single voice out of two strings.
What is this instrument we're stretched upon?
Who is the player that has us in his hands?
Such a sweet song.

DISORDERED (RESPONSE TO RILKE)

> *'so mächtig und ungeduldig ist mein Verlangen nach Ordnung'*
> *'so powerful and impatient is my desire for order'*
> — Rilke, Milanese letters

Over and over the same thing
just a matter of innocent repeating
and all will be uniform

Never mind the ragged edges
that improbable moon
will soon be full again

trailing disorder but in a manner
wholly cyclical, so sickening
to find in nature and 'human nature'

the justification of your own desire
though I cannot love chaos either —
these are two halves of the one

circle, each *das halbe Leben*, a face
beaming back at you what you project
and I reject the aesthetics of clockwork

too, the metrical turn — I want to happen
across words like a finishing, fallible
streak, one more minor disintegration

among the millions and who cares if we are
out of order so long as we can love each other
not fearing reverberation like strings on your

violin, nor longing for dark and silent spaces
but giving a big bright fiddler's hickey to
whoever holds us and is playing us if he's there

IRISH LIGHT

And yet it does come
intermittent
soft as new skin
and that vulnerable

warm with the knowledge
that warmth is
never permanent
and must be cossetted

this rare shadow-play
across the blinds
every branch haloed
a moment only

I make them slant
to admit it but
sunshine won't
come inside

that would need
utter openness
the neighbours' gaze
in such a labile place

but grateful for the least
lifting in the day's
mood, this sudden
silvering-over, little

apparitions I long for

FOR MY LATE AND FORMER TEACHER

You always found something more
to show me, shed light on, as if it
couldn't be helped, as if no matter what
we did, over a decade, to shift it
from this foot to that, rearrange
some shared mental furniture,
we were fixed in one relation:
I still had things to learn. And I do.
Now you continue, demonstrating
just what a year means, the ache, the worth,
the heft of it — even the empty weight:
this year of you gone.
                        But please go on,
pay no heed to interruption —
when the day's late and you really ought
to get home, students will always hold you back
          with one last question.

EDGE

> *the grave is a magnet*
> *that switches polarity*
> *when you reach it.*
> — John Kinsella

No seven-league boots but more like
leaky boats, these useless shoes
I'm sinking in, crossing the bleak lawn
to an ever-encroaching dark: each oak
nominally to mark another lost loved one
laid to rest herein, yet massing to form
a would-be woodland, phalanx I face down
seeking an actual name, a pair of dates.
Oakfield Wood, even the place-name's not
unique, I had to pick it out, and the man
who keeps tabs for visitors saw to it your spot
was flagged with a knotted plastic bag, bellyaching
at the wind's rough tug, yet not enough, since they all
sprang flags for someone, small tree-mast the only
weak vertical of this eroded tumulus, makeshift vessel,
dreaded horizontal, listing to Lethe, the Stour so near,
plied and polluted. I trudge along, recusant weaving
a way through pews of dirt, dank aisles of a roofless
and stripped cathedral, mere air where a spire might rise,
underfoot altogether too open, too permeable, lacking the slab's
hard border or marble's smug rebuff, tread back over old sod
like someone pacing the lines of a page that wobble and halt,
that state their writer wants to leave no traces, only merge
with earth and sky and water.

SHED

Sharpness is in there
and no mother.

Scarier than
her kitchen drawer.

A long dark door
I mustn't enter

unless Dad takes me.
I like it better,

paint-tray bigger
than dustpan, plane-

blade brighter
than any grater.

He tells my brother
Don't touch that

it's hot mate.
White paint is peeling.

He uses the hotmate
to blow off paint

teaches me
undercoat,

explains the layers
mixes colours.

I sit in the dirt,
don't need to be told

Don't touch
adoring the bubble

that can't get out,
the block he uses

to make things straight
that he calls *spirit*

level. Shows me *plumb*
and lets me play

with sandpaper like
a face unshaven

unfolded from pouch
of oily apron

loaded with nails
like the million pins

in Mum's sewing box
but nails are serious:

I know from threats
of rust-and-tetanus,

they melt and sink
under his claw hammer

which can also yank
them back, can make

your thumbnail
turn black: *get back.*

Smitten, I weigh
smooth wood

of hammer
and axe-handle

when he's not looking,
hold my breath at

loud axe-head
biting the red

stump of wood *get back*
get back as the chips

sting my bare legs
because I love

the smell of sap
the same way

clippings fly
damp and rich

hitting and nipping me
as he mows the lawn.

We follow on
when he sits down

for a drink
after a hard day's work

one on each knee:
my brother and me

until he begins to smoke
and sets us at his feet

for fear of ash
for safety's sake,

brown bottles poke
from a paper bag

soggy at edges,
he sings of a clock

that stopped short never
to go again

EVAPORATIVE WATER COOLER

God knows where he rustled it up from.
There was always the back of a truck, friend of a friend,
or some prospect he'd warmed up who came good,
some favour he'd called in, *silver-tongue, touch of the blarney*
and there it was, dripping, glittery, our high-ceilinged
weatherboard lounge-room set fluttering, all ears
for its rumbling, gravel-throated hum, and him
filling the back of the thing with a hose, great guzzler
that it was, lifting the fly-strips like something redemptive,
sending the ravaged pages of newsprint she hated flying
till we kids pounced barefoot on them, tamping
them down, rolling the toppled stubbies, and him
flaking out in the fat armchair, a snore to rival the growl
of the new secondhand cooler, us clustered at his feet,
and her resolute in the kitchen, the household settling
into temporary respite, cool spell, artificial and moveable
as temper sweltering that December, quelling the angst,
the discord of *coming down in the world*, a bought peace, barely
paid-for truce, running up bills he could always delay
or talk his way out of, still better than meltdown.

VIEW FROM BELOW

Though I grew up in the underlip of many dams
hills brimming with them, shimmering bodies
of illusion, endless founts of distribution, silver
of recumbent pipelines at one with the spectral uprights
of trees flown by at night when reclined in the back
of a ghost-grey Holden Premier station wagon, untrammelled
child-light, not having to drive but being driven, at leisure
to ponder — how we would haunt them, hardly real unless
we checked and rechecked this precious hoard of levels: Sunday
jaunt through catchment, parkland picnic, pictures courting
with concrete curve and railing for scenic backdrop, all to make us
happen, never a moment doubting the pledge to hold, the skill
or vigilance that kept them, like all things, in position, with the gleam
of fact, the preordained, what we had earned, as we imagined, seamless,
unstained, with barely a thought for the strain, the uphill struggle
their bulk, their burden, must mean — though we knew it was dryland,
our corner, but sheer heft of presence outweighed the debt,
yet here, in a once-wet country now too in drought, this wearing down
with doubt, so I can't abide to be anywhere I know is lower, downstream
of weir or reservoir, conscious they bear down like something that begs
delivery, sensing them just so much contestation I am, like everyone,
reliant on, and yet resenting that; aware of gravity as an indifferent force,
aware of the vast loss for every valley flooded, not only human movement
but chaos for other animals on every scale, for plants, sunken rot that will not
the way of all flesh for want of oxygen, but put out yet more carbon, so that w
can never win, sly erosion from sediment-hunger, the whole abnormal course
of it an ironic shot at the idea of trickle-down effect; the arch or edge
we teeter on, at mercy of only-too-human inspection that nurses its one
potent moment of neglect or inattention, and even should it never happen, th

unbearable pressure of awareness, that it is there above us, Titanic in reverse, monument to hubris, mass blank and smooth, irrefutable and refusing purchase like the very spillway surface, unleashed upon us before we would even know.

SENSITIVE

for Jean-François Samlong

Everything shut will open again:
the intimate green we don't notice
till you show us in this childhood place
how each leaf responds to the least
reading of fingertips, folding down,
as if we only briefly crossed its mind,
and were then forgotten
in its restoration:
Mimosa pudica, essence of discretion,
fragility of interface. Our touch
passes like cliff-shadow, leaving no trace.
Everything is a game, you say,
as the boy keeps leaping, will leap forever
into the spray beside the steep cascade,
imprint also effaced as he runs
back into daylight, evaporation.
What am I saying, thirty years!
It's forty, or fifty already. The ground
full of holes that are never sated, the road
an eternal ford with no sign of the other
side. Everything shut will open.

ABSCISSION

Something has stripped the green
from our walk   at Crookhaven

No more of nook or bower
nor tunnel to speak of

No leafy echo buffers
long-gone communications

A decisive break
A sealing-over

Where are those softer features
we knew the way by

Easy for those accustomed
lifelong to this mood-swing

But for a numb interior
stranger to fluctuation

The shock   the mirror
In bare twig and gaping vista

This is not what we came for

LIFE IN WATER

1

Talk about how many hours
we spend sleeping

Most of the earth's surface
is this   & does not know us

is like God in negative
theology   outside us

whatever we say of it
is meaningless

And yet we test it
prodding with one nervous

toe at cosmic coldness
or plunging headlong   hubris

Does swimming resemble
flying in dreams   something

certain but lost to the woken
or do we fly in dreams

because we recall water

2

I set my sandals neatly
near the steps   enter
a temple   no Siloam
descend to an underworld

But I don't go under
I keep face up
becoming no more than
head & shoulder

like my father
(long gone now)
who went so far
out we children thought

it was another order
always he needed space
and the ocean had more
than you looked for

touching shores
we scarcely credited
that he called
rest of the world

he said we must not follow
there was rip tide
and dark fin
he was beyond them

we called & called him
he stayed out longest
all on his own
Do as I say & not as I do

He told us
never to swim
in an empty place
it was a bad sign

Here in the small pond
indoor and heated
the sign says
you must go clockwise

like draining away
but nobody else is in
so I move at cross
purposes   a particle

erratic   & loop like
that second hand
on the wall   sweeping
insanely above the pool

where nobody cares
for personal best
there's none to witness
shame or success

3

There are others
who come here
at quiet times

we overlap
they are stripping
as I am dressing

I say hello
over one shoulder
make no

eye contact
it is enough
that we dip

into the same
trough   we don't
want to

wallow in it
My time is up
One day I'm sure

I'll have to share
these few
square feet of

weightlessness but
just for now I want
to keep up

the illusion

4
Once
to move like this
caused me no stress
it was second nature

but time's crept into
each interstice
like something embedded
encoded   I push against

the argument
in my own flesh
arms that could nurse
the deadweight

of infant sleep
without complaint
now ache at mere water
Water forgets the rest of me

but not my heavy
head   the neck that jerks
to retain control
just when I think

I'm wholly surface
I become no more than
this suspended thing
belonging

in neither element
my bulky meaning
not smooth or streamlined
not free of tension

making drag & splitting
what would include me
parted before me
as if I would pray

or wipe away
what's coming
kick it behind
and let it close over

After each aimless lap
I pause for breath
and turn   boustrophedon
that's soon erased

that no one's reading
yet every so often
the guards lean to the glass
make sure I'm still with them

note my position
when last seen
total abandon or
dead man's float

FOR MY FATHER

Somehow you're here

in each stroke
guiding my line
to the end —

in ease, surrender
my limbs remember
how you stood over

every departure
each risky venture
anything outdoor

your domain
we took it as power
to curb, to hinder

but now I am older

I see you there
from the earliest stumble
coaxing the opening gambit

dropping us into the deep
to provoke survival
by dog-paddle

just as you later
when I got L-plates
took me out before dawn

on empty roads
onto and off the gravel verge
potholes, corrugations

to hammer in
what you called
defensive driving

because you were adamant
they'd never train
or test for that

always alert to the mean
trick, the dark spot
where hazard could lurk

wanted, desperate,
to coach us, lifeguard
at water's edge

from the vantage point
of a knowledge
we couldn't yet have

that had pushed you,
spurred you, all your life
for some good reason

meant for bequeathing
or handing on, like a baton
the secret piece

of information
that would outwit
whatever was after us.

SEVENTH SWIM

When the man with the white beard
I mistook for a mask last week
comes again, I choose to stay in.

Wordless, a half-wave.
I move over, leave him the better part
keeping the steps.

He must remember how I bolted
that time, guessing at modesty
perhaps, but it isn't that.

Done with the idle float
the emptying-out of thought
now I must seem to swim.

Company means laps
invisible lines drawn up
not being yourself.

Awkward, unsteady
we push off from the same end
like two who start to speak

at the same moment
someone must overpower
or someone back down.

Yet it only takes
my natural languor
though younger, my weakness

to put us at odds without effort.
Soon we are opposites
crossing at midpoint

trying to double the space
but that is useless:
he makes a big stroke

sending his wake
across till I nearly choke
unused to this other rhythm

sets his face to the depth
and musters a lungful
coursing the whole length.

Even with one long side
ostensibly mine, I can't compete.
If this were a boat, it would tip.

STAUNCH

Why is she here, daily,
so clearly unwilling
to *do* anything
with the water? If this
is a mirror, it's blurred,
for a minute without
my glasses I think it's me
but she's only my size
and vintage, looks thoroughly fit,
and yet she's content to inch,
timid, back and forth like
sweeping under a fluid
carpet, each weak stroke
holding back some part
to state: *it's not my element*
valiant only in keeping
her face unsmudged and after
at most ten minutes, in getting out.

SOMETIMES

Sometimes they come back
the old usages

Words that were overlaid
but will out

The natural accent
Sole to the pedal

to freewheel
barefoot   upright

down the long hill
you were forbidden

Grit in the ball-bearings
of strap-on skates

you had to keep hidden
Or the exact momentum

for shinning up
the oak with no low

branches & just how
far out you could straddle

that limb without dipping
The splintery bits   the spots

milling with ants
Ammoniac stab of water at

the top of the nostril
Feel of the cartwheel

Push of the soil
at your walking hands

Catch of the soil
when you fall

Earthworms up close
glistening   shifting

grain by grain
to remake the garden

A cluster of pulses
like those you sought

at wrist   at temple
for bored amusement

as if they were separate
unstoppable   & had no count

All of this pig-Latin
your distant idiom

TRANSIENCE

Do I hallucinate

egret in paddock
steps ever tentative

upon a layer
never seen before

water so sudden
it can't sink in

but sits on the moment
like a new dimension —

mirage-egret, won
trophy already

dulled and doubted.

SELF-SUPPLY

1. Non-drinker

At the city
book launch:
Gallows Gallery,
slick planes and light-
lulled surfaces

where the only choice
is red or white
I ask discreetly
for water.

In the kitchen,
a host, apologetic:
hope you don't mind
straight from the tap.

I tell her
when you're off-scheme
that seems like
nectar.

2. Bathtub

Hypothetical, this shell,
part of a harmless
floor plan, selected back when
we hadn't yet been broken in.

Lily-bright, naïve,
useless as washed-up bone:
call it ornament if you like
or a vestigial organ
in the house's evolution.

Quite unchristened.
Only ever filled with dust
I must keep up with,
or made to drain
mop-dregs;

at best, to nest the meagre bowl
in which I hand-wash everything
that used to go in the machine.

3. Mains

How quickly the slack attitude clicks
back into place, as if it were always

like this, laid on, as if to the manner born.
How quickly the guilt of easy use

now dissipates, the body calls up these
rhythms of access, recourse.

I was washing my salads in bowls.
I was cleaning my teeth with a glass.

One week and recidivist. Somebody else
can do the penance for me, surely

Somebody else is plumbing it in.

4. Doing the Maths

Thirty-thousand kilometres
of water mains
and we're not on them.
A pipeline five hundred
and sixty-six kilometres long
with extensions north and south
that do not reach us.

A twenty-percent decline in rainfall
by the time I am sixty-six.
How many ten-litre water packs
from the local IGA
will I manage to carry by then?

My son will be twenty-seven.
He may just remember
when the block was green.
He may just remember
jam tree, York gum, sandalwood,
the olive grove across the road.

A forty-percent decline in rainfall —
I shall, if I'm lucky, be ninety-six.
If at all, then not staggering
down Coondle's steep slopes;
long past lugging things home
from the shops.

My son will be fifty-seven,
this block beyond what I can imagine,
beyond even the projection
of *Water Forever*'s fifty-year plan.

5. Neighbours

Sound in this valley rings
as if in an empty tank —

distance is not as private
as you think.

Way off on the nearest block
is Mick, pitching small talk

by weird acoustics
across the great gap

to John, other side of the gully,
who asks, *Did you check*

your rain gauge — how many mils?

Eighteen years in this dry place
getting drier, Mick calls

back, *Nah, I never look*
till I turn on the tap

and nothing comes out.

6. Parish Pump

In Town is *on scheme*.
Outside is not.
You can place residents
by stress or nonchalance.

Too much more dry
and Outside is calling
Aquarius in,
straining up hilltops

for a steep fee
nobody likes
to admit they've stumped up
but at the bus stops

their children bluster
the price per litre
as if it were glamour
rather than failure.

In Town the woman
at the grocery counter
where I buy water
by the container

still makes the same crack
about fixing our tank
as if I were smiling
and it was a joke.

7. Scrutiny

Self-supply is a mirror in which you always look ugly.
You can squirm, but the reality slaps back at you:

it's not happening, the rain just isn't there.

When you turn on a scheme-tap you make a buffer.
Someone is out there looking after it, somebody somewhere.

You don't even have to see it to believe, you can feel the deep
pulse of the hidden god, all his arteries ground-embedded, stretching

to meet you in your purely human mundane, the one where
if you cut back on showers or hair-wash they'll complain at work
or if your lawn looks tired they'll say you're letting the street down.

He's a generous sort, this god, he knows you shouldn't have to be spartan,
got no time to deal with things, that's why you delegate, why you elect.

But self-supply says every outcome of your every action comes home to roc

Self-supply means you're a Catholic kid again examining your every fault,
except there's no one to absolve, you have to face yourself without recourse
to any collective comfort, any god.

They'll say: it's political, not personal,
not to be solved by the individual, which is true, but also less than the whol
truth, because this is no pool of Narcissus, this is the place where each actic

adds to each other action, where the mirage of distance from consequence
is swiftly dispelled, and the result is something closer to getting the picture

INTERRUPTUS

The world turns
differently at night.
Another order
kicks in.
There is a limit
to our mutual grasp
of habit, cohabitation:
outside, the kangaroos await
internal dark and silence,
thinking we've clocked off
because we are bedded down.
Or perhaps they do know
and consider us harmless
in this mode.
At the crucial moment,
distraction:
the mob pounds down
the hill, a mass release
beside the still,
breath-holding house.

PHEROMONAL

Other times they come
sniffing the windows

curious in excess,
no mere impulse

for safety, maybe
they want to know us

or are they incredulous

ADMISSION

I know it like your shadow
in all its variations
across the day

can always say
that is his footfall
although in fact it rises

and rises, your arrival
is part of you, a halo
of where you have been

and where you will go —
each imperfect cadence
brings you closer

though uncompleted.
What's at the top,
mute jacquemart,

Old Father Time?
Our days divided
now after years

in the same few rooms,
we're figurines
in a Black Forest

clock, rotate without
even touching — it's
cold in this stairwell

with windows no one
would open, snow-trail
that pools and flecks

each tread despite
the best intentions
however you wait

on winder, on landing,
you cannot shake
the dark, the noise

the outside coming in.

SHAKE-DOWN

While you are gone is always
the best time for laundering

I can be housewife
unselfconscious

outside roles
in a borrowed place.

This thing that covers us
must be whipped off

no more procrastination!
A starting-again.

I shuck off the skin:
fake leopard, the sort of thing

some keep for the bedroom
— downstairs is Nice.

Never our choice
but we live with it.

Inside is white, forgetful
tabula rasa, our cloud

of unknowing, a nightly
draining, day's residue.

Flat mundanity you keep
neat as a slab, a plot

now let loose from the bed
grows monstrous, voluminous

bulking beyond me so I tread
gingerly, feeling for steps

I cannot see, am top-heavy,
comical, cartoon's moving tree

till I reach the machine & strain
to cram it in, my bloated

evil twin, my almost weightless
burden. And after the whole mess,

the wrestle, the tussle of getting
this dead placenta to fit back in.

CEILING

You're meant to lance it
With Phillips-head
Concede defeat
For the moment

The way blood's let
To stave off greater
Bloodshed, disaster
Coax thin thread

Into truce-bucket
Preventive measure
Against mass water
Against the force

Of what we've prayed for
(With tank near-empty)
And would hold back now
Allow, not fight it

Pointless to staunch
With weak interior
Taking and taking
While outside breach

Over your head
Goes undetected
Instead, you spread
Each plastered finger

As if to feel for pulse or flutter
And paste your mess
Like salve or poultice
In one last gesture

Of trust or educated
Guess, based on what's
Held till now and should
Go on holding.

SIEGE

I've grown used to this:
the tap, the rattle —
learned to dismiss
the insistence, and say

the raven, near mating,
mistaking his reflection
for some insufferable rival
who must be neutralised

at once, cracking his fragile
self-image, exact match,
prising up tiles like scales
or flakes of my skin as I feel

this house begin to fit me
impervious, I trust, hoping
he makes no headway,
almost successfully

fending off incursion
or even the suggestion
that I am in any way
at risk, indifferent, convinced

these rumblings mean nothing,
so that I wholly miss deliveries
intended, the postie, for instance
rapping insanely, trying repeatedly

and finally giving up on me.

SECOND SIEGE

It begins by night
when you think to be private,
that nothing can call you out

but this brazen gale
lays waste to all
willed peace or rest;

you toss, lost vessel,
and roll, and reconsider
what you are doing here —

had you forgotten
these soul-winters, the way
they strike and blight every

good intention — yet
yours is a strong house, stone
and slate, and every creak

already accounted for
through many a bleak year
that still in turn saw summer

and should see more,
nothing that lies loose or
unmastered about this place

so why the blank ache, paralysis
at a merely exterior shriek
as if it might herald collapse

and all you can do is wait?

CUSP

It starts in dreams
a full cupboard, forgotten,
wardrobe tumbling open
no matter how much you've packed.
And a new distance, rehearsed
mentally lifting skirts an inch
above the mud so as not to trail
associations home. Not following
loosely with warmth but seeing
things everywhere congeal, or freeze,
aesthetic and protective, since love cannot
be temporary. Objects become only
what's for storing — already they wear
their coating — food is for *eating down*.
No more mail orders, you will not
be here, no acquisitions bigger
than your pocket. Everything laundered,
put back where it was. The house
will revert to behaving as someone else's.
No imprint taken. They won't even know
you are gone.

THE KINDLING

Matchstick, where lean and stripling do not equal
inconsequential; matchstick, whose tendency to snap
is all that saved a huddle of small boys from what they
wanted to know, yesterday at school, slender but potent
treasure neglected on the art-room floor, detected
by these sharp lads, and one of them was him, our son,
whom we think we know, who prides himself on
commonsense, whom we call *smart* and *bright*, a flame
that wavers between arrogance and self-belief, a glow
you wouldn't want put out but which could flare and go
either way if you lost control of it; matchstick I know
from his description though he wasn't quite certain,
having never actually held one, as if possessed by joy
of the sort that cannot believe its luck, glee that straightens
the face to say *I would never* but will still seek to spark
the day after, when his father is lighting the woodstove
and he craves to watch despite stern injunction, *I just
wanted to see, I just wanted to see if it was the same ...*

PROSPECT

Crown of hills tender with green and dandelion
gold, but baffled on one side with slate of storm cloud.
In the crest of sun you can still see what's coming.

Twice daily I perch here to meet the school bus,
brash streak of orange through the other side
of the valley: climbing, dipping, suddenly upon me.

Winter like this I sit in the car. Summer I walk up here,
punishing muscle, light so austere I have to stop in the one
jam tree's one shade patch, and wait for my son. Afternoon:

the neighbours' children step off, each one holding down
fence-wires to let the next one into the hillside
grazing-paddock and down to their low-nested house.

Morning: we watch them loom as their ute mounts the drive
and the small daughter leaps out to handle the gate,
in rehearsal for a life of it, on a block just like this, the way

her father would also have done on his distant farm
in childhood; like him also, the two boys ride on the tray-top,
wind ripping hair as if it were heads of wild oat and wheat,

tall and short, rigid, alert, standing there gripping the bar
like gymnasts limbering up for their life of it too, and when
the ute swings, they never fall, they know how to lean with it.

THE GRASS-CUTTER

Strange interlude, this week or more
once a year, in which he puts on

the old gear, black like his daily wear
but thicker, stiffened, coated by grease,

grass-tips and general grime, same as
last time, hair-shirt or scarecrow-garb

he calls iron maiden and must shower
even before, so as to feel vaguely human

flinching at texture ripe as old rot,
a living shroud, the dross and refuse

of our block so woven in, laid as sediment
within the garment, fossil record, too far gone

to wash in the machine, so it sits there, all year
waiting for him, too thin for armour, lets

in darts and shots that the ground retorts
in their annual tête-à-tête, the Place of Stones

whose steep slope no mower can take, combat
hand-to-hand but who's the opponent? not

this land, not jam tree or York gum, that get
the blame if a spark should fly ... Our neighbour

Jay says *Everyone here just uses spray*, the 'quick'
solution, compounding the problem, for *everyone*

also drinks from bores and tanks and no one
thinks of the consequence and so he's out there,

John, in that crazed casing, razing the dry wild oats,
making us fit as he can for the feared fire season

that is always to come, doing it hard, meeting each
stalk the same way God reportedly counts each hair

of your head, each sparrow that falls, alive to this patch
of six acres as only such work can make you, all he can do.

THE DOUBLE APPOINTMENT

Taking our turn each to enter
this dark cabinet as if it were
confessional, only the failings are
ocular, commonplace and we hope
venial not mortal; in any case this

master's scrutiny dispenses no
sacrament, merely lenses. And graven
images: a new machine that can scan
and fathom inside the eye, rotated
in three dimensions — look, my

macula as it should be, relief, he
calls you in from your pew to see,
returned to privacy: *your wife in a way you've
never seen before*, not louche but humorous,
charting the way we, so close, share the loss

of hold on the outside world — a pair
of old shoes or trousers still together
in decline as in all else — and yet treasure
each other no less. *Look at that membrane,
floating, detached!* he says, *detached*, and your

question leaps anxious but it is nothing
serious, just my vitreous ageing
along with the rest of us, and now for weeks
you will have to drive me, go wherever
I need to go, just as I'd do for you if you were

this helpless, extending each other's senses,
flesh-of-my-flesh prosthetic, bone-of-my-bone
symbiosis, until my new set is ready to collect
and I'll be once more communicant, outwardly
focussed, appearing to manage all by myself.

THE WATER BEARER

1

To live in the mountain's shadow, find my way
to crook of world's arm, back to the point where
a soul's reinvented, light of old saint never sainted,
poet born there, who graced it with first words, small Adam:
Oh colour Oh sun Oh joli

What a child could see, what the mother noted
with that fine bright attention only a parent can shine
on the word, the sign, the sound; how later, back in America,
her boy still rang with churchbells of the Pyrenean foothills:
Dah-hou   Dah-hou

Homesick for somewhere I'd never been, though close,
in the many ideas that blend into one like the rivers
descending to confluence, Conflent, a region, a name
not to be real for me, how could I say: I want to go home?
Abandoned, like plans. *That world was the picture of Hell*

the adult poet wrote, and it *was* Hell, but he meant to lead
to his own conclusions, a road through the tangle of heathers
and wars, through the dark unnamed and personal wrongs
that brought him, midway his way of life, to the monastery:
Our real journey in life is interior

2

Led to my first error: for want of Trappists, trying
the Carmelites — feeble and florid, I lasted a summer,
transplanted and underwatered. Imagine the confines

where nothing's written without permission, imagine
scraps of cardboard saved from packs of socks and stockings,
covert with poem-scrawl I couldn't show the Sisters

but slipped out, surreptitious, through parlour bars
clear sign, had I known it, of the wrong vocation,
poet maybe despite me, but I was no Merton.

Distracted by the gory stories of evening Recreation,
the way the Extern brought them in, dredging tabloids. Fazed
by the Prioress avidly reading a letter, forensic

on the exhumation of *dear departed* sisters from the yard
of an old Carmel in New South Wales that would merge
with another Carmel, there being so few new postulants

these secular-minded days. Small wonder. The more I worried,
the more I signed off on my own doom, the night the Novice
Mistress handed back my crumpled civvies, and banned goodbyes.

In my bare-floored flat once more on the outside, I sent the poems off.
I named them after impossible water drawn from Isaiah.
And David who wrote, *My soul thirsts for God.*

I wanted psalms but all I could muster was meter.
I'm still here, still thirsty, still wince at that first reviewer
lamenting, *utterly without irony.*

Years later a Sister, on reading my books, said
piously, meaning it kindly, *Only the mentally stable
can manage Carmel.*

3
How to come into the world
and not decry it — I re-read
The Seven Storey Mountain
nearly thirty years later
and wonder how it could ever

have knocked me over, how did
those first lines more than hook
me in? The doctrine? I was twenty-one.
Now I see only a young man
trying to fit in, zealously keen

in his newly Catholic skin
to abjure every good thing
he once took delight in,
with the poet deep in him
bucking and chafing for

one last sin, the beauty of so-called
Creation he *has* to see as fallen
still seducing him, Augustine
and his *But not yet*. Unconvincing,
more to everything than he's letting on.

POEM FOR SHROVE TUESDAY

It was an upright coffin
but latticed for breathing

it was the first step
into a trap   a cabriolet

lurching journey
that went nowhere

began & finished
at the same dead-end

same old exchange where
you'd both pretend to be strangers

what kind of ear could crave
that training in scruples

at six years old?
& always a bit withheld

not from intention
but because there were

no words for it
the part of you kept in

which was not sin
& he knew that

When you were twelve
they made changes

started the face-to-face
but still you sat side

by side & avoided
each other's eyes

You wanted the box back
the stiffness of artifice

form's protection
anything but this

POEM FOR ASH WEDNESDAY

How his thumb smudged it on
like marking a page
for later reading

exactly the way
the checkout man
licks & swipes to open

a bag that won't cooperate
when the queue's endless
— so many penitents!

He was teaching a posture
a mode of carriage
to fix it there

only the smoothest
uncreased brow
could bear witness

What you are and
where you're going
you will remember

CROSSING MYSELF

The stoup at the door is empty.
Our Lady of Knock reduced to a pun.
Somebody else's house I call home
on borrowed time. I know the routine.
An empty stoup, God-shaped.

I could fill it myself from the tap:
base water, Tess baptising Sorrow.
Or savour the void it cradles, knowing
though hands may be trained to mere pattern,
no power holds, no priest steers me,

nor ever will step inside again to belabour,
upbraid a mother's unsainted rooms,
the way she hid the hated objects
in a father's absence. Nor to badger
a frightened child with limbo.

The stoup's too small for grown fingers.
They itch like stitches, yet find it wanting.
Not even dried relic of sponge, no hyssop
to soothe Christ's lip, to slow the loss, the attrition.
Only this cracked plastic shell, with nothing to offer.

Though it lodge in the brain and beg for
response, I repeat: it is empty — no drop will grace
my ingressions, transgressions, nor register
deference as if I clocked on. My left hand knows
        what my right hand is doing.

ACKNOWLEDGEMENTS

Some of the poems in this collection were first published in the *Australian Book Review, Australian Poetry Journal, Axon, the Canberra Times, The Arc-Cordite Poetry Special Issue, Dazzled: the University of Canberra Vice Chancellor's International Poetry Prize Anthology 2014, Eureka Street, The Kenyon Review, Mascara Literary Review, Southerly, This Corner, The Warwick Review, The Weekend Australian,* and *Writ Poetry Review.*

The poem 'The Water Bearer' contains allusions to the autobiography of Thomas Merton, writer and Cistercian monk, who was born under the sign of Aquarius, January 31, 1915.

Thanks to the Literature Board of the Australia Council for a grant to write many of these poems, and to the Literary Cultures of the Global South program, University of Tübingen, Germany, where many were also written.

ALSO AVAILABLE FROM FREMANTLE PRESS

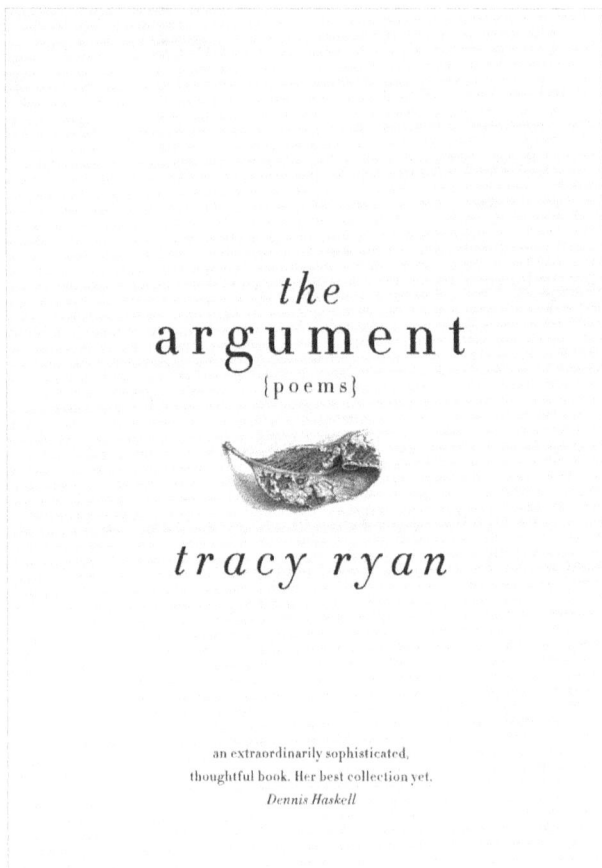

the
a r g u m e n t
{p o e m s}

t r a c y r y a n

an extraordinarily sophisticated,
thoughtful book. Her best collection yet.
Dennis Haskell

Tracy Ryan is a poet 'writing at the height of her powers'
Alison Croggon.

'The language of *The Argument* is taut, whittled down, spare ... This is
poetry richly grounded in the real, yet alive to its
fluctuating uncertainty.' *Andrew Taylor*

ONLINE AT WWW.FREMANTLEPRESS.COM.AU

ALSO AVAILABLE FROM FREMANTLE PRESS

Tracy Ryan at her mature and forensic best.
– *Geoff Page*

An achievement of the highest order from
one of Australia's most gifted poets.
– *Marion May Campbell*

An astonishing work; nothing less
than a poetry of life and death.
– *David McCooey*

UNEARTHED

TRACY RYAN

'The dead – or the living – require the respect of our attention, as does
this humane and remarkable book.' *Cordite Poetry Review*

'Once again, Ryan reveals herself as poet with both a clear sense of
tradition – and a contemporary understanding of Ezra Pound's old
injunction to "Make it new!"' *Geoff Page*

AND AT ALL GOOD BOOKSTORES

First published 2018 by
FREMANTLE PRESS
25 Quarry Street, Fremantle 6160
(PO Box 158, North Fremantle 6159)
Western Australia
www.fremantlepress.com.au

Cover image Herzstaub/www.shutterstock.com
Printed by Lightning Source

National Library of Australia
Cataloguing-in-Publication entry

Ryan, Tracy, 1964–, author
The water bearer / Tracy Ryan
Australian poetry.
Water—Poetry.
ISBN 9781925164954 (pbk)

Department of
Local Government, Sport
and Cultural Industries

GOVERNMENT OF
WESTERN AUSTRALIA

lotterywest
supported

Fremantle Press is supported by the State Government through the
Department of Local Government, Sport and Cultural Industries.

Australian Government

Australia
Council
for the Arts

Publication of this title was assisted by the Commonwealth Government
through the Australia Council, its arts funding and advisory body.